L–5.5/P–0.5

JOHN PAUL JONES

AMERICAN NAVAL HERO

TRACIE EGAN

rosen central

Primary Source™

The Rosen Publishing Group, Inc., New York

Published in 2004 by The Rosen Publishing Group, Inc.
29 East 21st Street, New York, NY 10010

Copyright © 2004 by The Rosen Publishing Group, Inc.

Library of Congress Cataloging-in-Publication Data

Egan, Tracie.
John Paul Jones / Tracie Egan.
    v. cm. — (Primary sources of famous people in American history)
Includes bibliographical references and index.
Contents: A life at sea—The Revolutionary War—The Bonhomme Richard—Life after the war.
ISBN 0-8239-4113-2 (library binding)
ISBN 0-8239-4185-X (pbk.)
6-pack ISBN 0-8239-4312-7
1. Jones, John Paul, 1747–1792—Juvenile literature. 2. Admirals—United States—Biography—Juvenile literature. 3. United States. Navy—biography—Juvenile literature. 4. United States—History—Revolution, 1775–1783—Naval operations—Juvenile literature. [1. Jones, John Paul, 1747–1792. 2. Admirals. 3. United States—History—Revolution, 1775–1783—Naval operations.] I. Title. II. Series.
E207.J7E37 2004
973.3'5'092—dc21

                                                          2002154991

Manufactured in the United States of America

Photo credits: cover © Stock Montage/SuperStock, Inc.; pp. 4, 18 © Private Collection/Bridgeman Art Library; p. 5 © The Pierpont Morgan Library/Art Resource, NY; p. 7 (top) courtesy of the Map Division, The New York Public Library, Astor, Lenox, and Tilden Foundations; p. 7 (bottom) © Dumfries Museum; p. 8 Library of Congress Geography and Map Division; p. 9 Library of Congress Prints and Photographs Division; p. 10 Library of Congress, Washington, D.C., USA/Bridgeman Art Library; pp. 11 (top), 25, 29 (top) © Bettmann/Corbis; p. 11 (bottom) Bibliotheque Nationale, Paris, France/Lauros-Giraudon-Bridgeman Art Library; pp. 13, 21, 23, 24 © Hulton/Archive/Getty Images; p. 14 Chateau de Versailles, France/Giraudon-Bridgeman Art Library; pp. 15, 16 National Archives and Records Administration; p. 17 Architect of the Capitol; p. 19 © SuperStock, Inc.; p. 20 Beinecke Rare Book and Manuscript Library/Yale University; p. 27 Museum of Tropinin and His Contemporaries, Moscow, Russia/Bridgeman Art Library; p. 28 © Burstein Collection/Corbis; p. 29 (bottom) Paul A. Souders/Corbis.

Designer: Tom Forget; Photo Researcher: Rebecca Anguin-Cohen

CONTENTS

1 A LIFE AT SEA

John Paul Jones was one of the most famous naval officers in American history. He helped lead America to victory during the Revolutionary War. He is credited with founding the United States Navy.

British troops arrive to occupy New York City in 1776, one of the events that marked the beginning of the American War of Independence.

A portrait of John Paul Jones as a young naval officer. A hero in the United States, he was considered a pirate in Britain.

John Paul was born on July 6, 1747, in Scotland. At an early age, John Paul became interested in ships and the sea. When he was 13 years old, he became a midshipman, an apprentice seaman, on board a merchant ship. John Paul's first job was on the *Friendship*, which traveled from England to Barbados in the West Indies and back.

A TRADITION OF REBELLION

John Paul Jones was originally from Scotland. The Scots have long resented being under English rule. It is not surprising that John Paul took the side of the colonists against England.

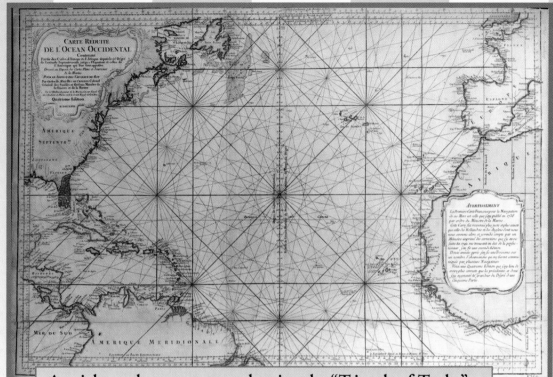

An eighteenth-century map showing the "Triangle of Trade," the exchange of slaves, sugar, rum, and goods that took place across the Atlantic Ocean. Below, the cottage where John Paul Jones was born in Kirkbean, Scotland.

When he was 21 years old, John Paul received his first command, the ship *John*. He spent many years as a successful merchant captain in the West Indies on the *John* and other ships. In 1773, he had to kill a mutinous sailor. To escape an angry mob, he decided to immigrate to the Virginia Colony in North America.

A map of the middle Atlantic colonies showing the colony of Virginia, where John Paul settled after commanding the *John*

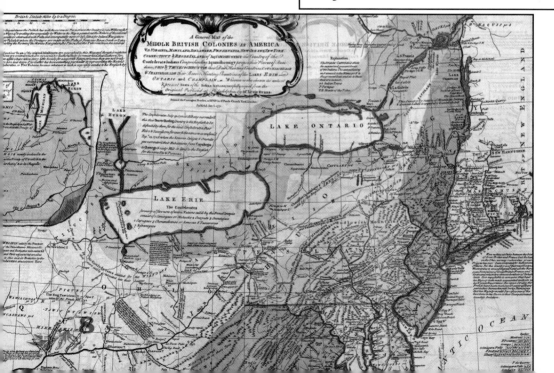

John Paul Jones's home in Fredericksburg, Virginia. The colony was three years away from declaring its independence from Britain when John Paul arrived.

At this time, the British government was taxing colonists in America. Many colonists believed it was unfair for England to tax them if they were not represented in the government. They were ready to fight for their freedom.

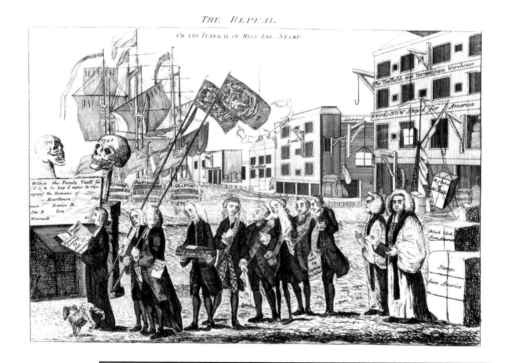

A satirical broadside shows a funeral procession for the Stamp Act, a tax on printed materials that England had to end as a result of colonial resistance.

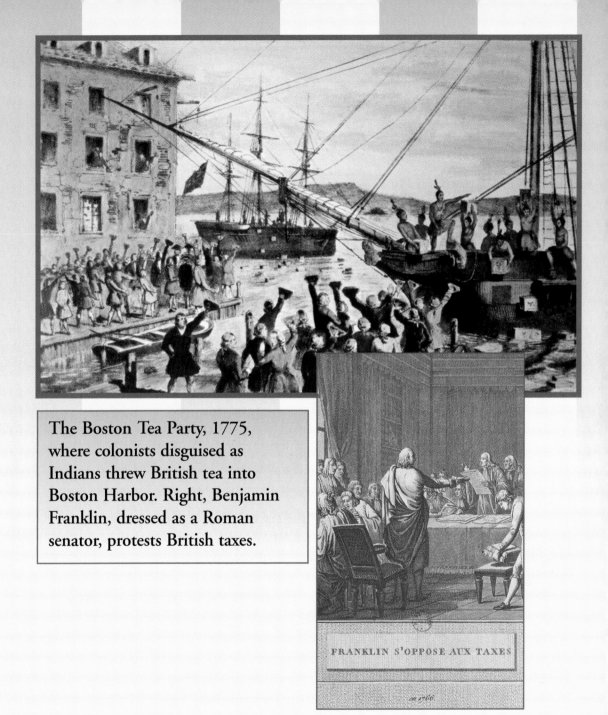

The Boston Tea Party, 1775, where colonists disguised as Indians threw British tea into Boston Harbor. Right, Benjamin Franklin, dressed as a Roman senator, protests British taxes.

FRANKLIN S'OPPOSE AUX TAXES

en 1766.

2 THE REVOLUTIONARY WAR

In December 1775, the Continental Congress made John Paul a lieutenant in the new American navy. As lieutenant on the ship *Alfred*, he was the first person to raise a flag that featured the red and white stripes that symbolized the resistance of the colonies to tyranny.

A FLAG FOR AMERICANS

The first American flag featured the Union Jack, the crossed bars of the British flag. When the British troops saw it, they thought that the Americans were surrendering. So George Washington ordered a new flag with thirteen stars instead.

Grand Union Flag 1776

The Grand Union Flag was the first American flag used by Washington's troops. The thirteen stars replaced the Union Jack in June 1777.

In August 1776, one month after the Declaration of Independence was signed in Philadelphia, John Paul was appointed captain of the 12-gun ship *Providence*. Under John Paul's command, the *Providence* captured or sank 40 British ships.

A naval battle in Chesapeake Bay during the Revolutionary War. In the age of sail, sea battles were often fought at close quarters.

The Declaration of Independence, 1776, written principally by Thomas Jefferson, gave the reasons that American colonists desired to be free of Britain.

In 1777, John Paul took command of the *Ranger*. He sailed to France, flying the new American flag on his ship, and brought word of General Burgoyne's surrender to American forces at Saratoga. This victory caused the French to support the American cause.

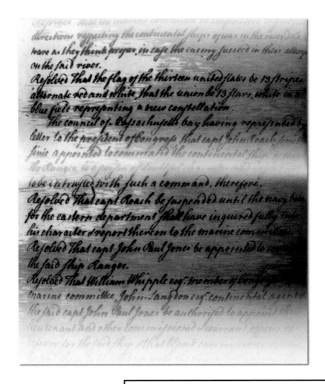

The resolution passed by Congress on June 14, 1777, authorizing a new flag with thirteen stars

The surrender of General Burgoyne to American general
Horatio Gates at Saratoga. In Paris, Benjamin Franklin secured
the support of the French king because of this victory.

In 1778, John Paul Jones and Admiral La Motte Piquet of the French navy exchanged gun salutes. It was the first salute of the American flag by a foreign warship. Later that year, John Paul sailed to the coasts of England and Scotland in the *Ranger* and captured more British ships, including the *Drake*.

The *Ranger* in action, commanded by John Paul Jones. The *Ranger* captured many British ships and disrupted commerce at English ports.

John Paul Jones unfurls the new American flag on the *Ranger*. It was probably Congressman Francis Hopkinson, not Betsy Ross, who designed the new flag.

3 THE *BONHOMME RICHARD*

In 1777, the French king gave John Paul an old merchant ship. Jones fixed it up and renamed it the *Bonhomme Richard* after *Poor Richard's Almanac*. Benjamin Franklin wrote *Poor Richard's Almanac*, and Jones named the ship in honor of Franklin, whom he admired.

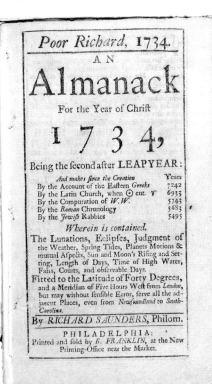

The title page from *Poor Richard's Almanack*, 1734, published by Benjamin Franklin. Franklin was the American ambassador to France during the Revolution.

The officers of the *Bonhomme Richard*, from a commemorative poster by Currier & Ives

On September 23, 1779, John Paul began his most famous battle. He attacked the British ship *Serapis* off the coast of England. Outgunned and badly damaged in the first exchange of fire, the *Bonhomme Richard* could not outshoot the *Serapis*. Jones brought his ship next to the *Serapis* and locked the two ships together.

JUMPING SHIP

John Paul Jones's ship, the *Bonhomme Richard*, was actually sinking when the British captain surrendered the *Serapis*. It went down two days after the engagement.

The sea battle between the *Bonhomme Richard* and the *Serapis*. Jones's aggressiveness, even in a sinking ship, won the day.

The *Bonhomme Richard* caught fire and began to sink. The captain of the *Serapis* saw this and called to John Paul. Would he surrender? John Paul's famous reply was "I have not yet begun to fight." John Paul used his remaining guns to damage the main mast of the British ship. The British captain lost his nerve and surrendered the *Serapis*.

A portrait of Captain Richard Pearson, commander of the *Serapis*

John Paul Jones calls out to the commander of the *Serapis* that he will not surrender.

4 LIFE AFTER THE WAR

John Paul Jones had many political rivals, and he never again held a high command in the American navy. In 1788, he was commissioned a rear admiral in the Russian navy by Empress Catherine II. He hoped that by commanding a battle fleet in Russia, he would earn a higher command back in America when the country built a permanent navy.

THE ADMIRAL COMES HOME

President Theodore Roosevelt admired John Paul Jones. In the early 1900s, he sent four ships to bring Jones's remains back to the United States. The ships were escorted up the Chesapeake Bay by seven battleships.

Catherine the Great, empress of Russia. John Paul Jones served in the Russian navy for a brief time.

John Paul was successful in the Russian navy, but jealous rivals forced him to leave. In 1790, he retired and moved to Paris. On July 18, 1792, he died. He was buried in Paris in an unmarked grave.

In 1913, his body was returned to the United States, and John Paul Jones was finally laid to rest in the U.S. Naval Academy Chapel in Annapolis, Maryland.

A bronze bust of John Paul Jones. In the Russian navy, he fought bravely in a campaign against the Turks.

A portrait of John Paul Jones in his naval uniform. Below, his marble sarcophagus under the Naval Academy Chapel in Annapolis, Maryland.

TIMELINE

1747—John Paul is born in Scotland on July 6.

1760—The 13-year-old John Paul becomes an apprentice on a merchant ship.

1768—John Paul receives his first command on the *John* when he is 21 years old.

1773—John Paul moves to the colony of Virginia in North America.

1775—In December, Jones is made lieutenant in the navy by the Continental Congress. He enters the Revolutionary War.

1778—Jones sails to France on the *Ranger*. On February 14, the American flag is saluted by the French.

1779—Jones attacks the *Serapis* with his ship, the *Bonhomme Richard*. He is victorious.

1788—Jones commands a Russian battle fleet for Empress Catherine II.

1790—Jones moves to Paris and retires.

1792—Jones is appointed U.S. consul to Algiers. A few months later, on July 18, he dies.

1913—Jones's body is removed from France and is buried in the U.S. Naval Academy Chapel in Annapolis, Maryland

GLOSSARY

apprentice (uh-PREN-tis) Someone who attaches himself or herself to a master at some profession in order to learn the business.

colony (CAHL-ah-nee) A settlement in a new country that is still controlled by another country.

lieutenant (loo-TEH-nent) A person in the military who ranks just below a captain.

merchant (MUR-chint) A person who buys, sells, and trades merchandise.

raid (RAYD) To make a sudden attack.

surrender (suh-REN-der) To lay down your weapons and recognize that your opponent has beaten you.

tax (TAKS) A sum of money that is taken from citizens by the government.

tyranny (TEER-uh-nee) A government in which those who are ruled have no rights or say in how they are governed.

WEB SITES

Due to the changing nature of Internet links, the Rosen Publishing Group, Inc., has developed an online list of Web sites related to the subject of this book. This site is updated regularly. Please use this link to access the list:

http://www.rosenlinks.com/fpah/jpjo

PRIMARY SOURCE IMAGE LIST

Page 4: *Disembarking of the English Troops at New York, 1776*, an engraving by Francois Xavier Haberman.

Page 5: Portrait of John Paul Jones, by an anonymous French painter, now with the Pierpont Morgan Library.

Page 8: Map of the American colonies, printed for Carington Bowles, London, 1771.

Page 9: John Paul Jones's house in Fredericksburg, Virginia. Photographed by Theodor Horydzak.

Page 10: *The Repeal of the Stamp Act*, an engraving published in 1766, now with the Library of Congress.

Page 11: *The Boston Tea Party*, a Currier & Ives lithograph. An engraving of Benjamin Franklin by David, now with the Bibliotheque National, Paris.

Page 14: *Naval Battle in Chesapeake Bay, September 3rd, 1781*. Painted in 1848 by Jean Antoine Chateau de Versailles.

Page 15: The Declaration of Independence.

Page 16: Congressional resolution, June 14, 1777.
Page 17: *The Surrender of General Burgoyne*, painted by John Trumbull, 1817, now in the rotunda of the Capitol Building.
Page 18: *The Ranger*, an engraving, 1793, by an anonymous English artist.
Page 19: *John Paul Jones Unfurling His Flag on the Ranger*, painted by Clyde O. Deland.
Page 20: *Poor Richard's Almanac*.
Page 21: The officers of the *Bohomme Richard*, a lithograph by Currier & Ives.
Page 23: The sea battle between the *Bonhomme Richard* and the *Serapis*.
Page 24: A portrait of Richard Pearson, captain of the *Serapis*.
Page 25: John Paul Jones aboard the *Bonhomme Richard*, from an undated painting.
Page 27: Portrait of Empress Catherine II of Russia by Fyodor Stepanovich Rokotov, now with the Museum of Tropinin and His Contemporaries, Moscow.
Page 29: A portrait of John Paul Jones, based on an etching by Moreau made in 1780 while Jones was still alive.

INDEX

ABOUT THE AUTHOR

Tracie Egan is a freelance writer who lives in New York City.